And I Just Kept On Walking

Amanda Ducksbury

Profits from this book are going to SAFA

SAFA Cumbria is a charitable organisation offering one to one and group counselling support to people aged 11 and above whom self harm in Cumbria. We offer much needed support, advice and guidance to family, friends and professionals. SAFA is a team of qualified staff committed to working positively with a wide range of self harm behaviours, such as: self-injury, sexual/risk taking behaviours, eating disorders, alcohol/substance/medication misuse and OCD.

Our primary goal is to empower the individual to take responsibility of their own lives by offering individual counselling and trusting support. We work to eliminate the stigma and discrimination associated with self-harm by creating greater awareness through training and education. We are very proud of the professional and creative work we do that has played and is playing such an important part in the recovery of so many people who self-harm. It is wonderful that Mandy has generously chosen to support us in our work through the creativity of her words, thank you.

Poetry © 2017 Amanda Ducksbury
Photography © 2017 Paul Ducksbury

First edition, Mar 2017

ISBN-13: 978-1542920681
ISBN-10: 154292068X

The journey has been bumpy with all the twists and turns life takes. It would be fair to say that my life hasn't been a bowl of cherries but I consider myself lucky though. After all life has put me through, I am still plodding on and am stronger for it. Discovering writing ten years ago, writing is a cathartic way of healing. I am at peace when I have a piece of paper and pen in my hand, writing as to whatever mood I am in. Depression hit me with all it's might and I couldn't see wood for the trees. The harder I tried to climb out of the pit I was in the further I fell backwards, until it spiralled out of control. Gradually with the right help, some beautiful walks and good friendships I was able to just keep on walking.

Dedication

To my husband Paul with love and thanks for all your help. My friends Grace, Beryl, Mary and Sue for their continued support and friendship without whom I wouldn't have ever believed I could come this far with my writing. Also Sue, Helene and Kevin for making life more bearable and making me believe in myself. Thanks to everyone else who have helped me on my journey. And last but not least, love and thanks to my dear Dad.

Contents

Despair and Hope

Deep in the depths of despair
I seem to sink lower and lower
The blackness engulfs me
It would seem that there is no way out

I am walking and I just keep on walking.
I find the gift of being able to write
I pick myself up and seek some help
cherish my friendships
and just keep on walking on my journey.

Gradually the dark cloud starts to lift
I discover the fells and the beauty of the countryside
I find inner peace and start to relax and enjoy life.

Tongue Gill, Grasmere

SPRING

Blencathra

Hellvelyn

Walking up Sticks Pass
on this beautiful sunny morning
pockets of frost lay on sheltered fields.

The steep path meandered it's way up the fell side
loose stone making it difficult to get a grip.
The hum of the traffic in the distance
one of the only sounds to be heard.

Snow still covered parts of the mountain
as winter tries to cling on.
Approaching the top, the wind got stronger.
Breathtakingly beautiful at the summit.

The cool waters of Red Tarn looking inviting
on this warm spring day
The view from the summit goes on forever.

The Sea

The sea shimmering silver in the moonlight
Whispers softly in the silence of the night.
The lullaby of the tide ebbing and flowing
the rhythm of the waves soothing.
The moonlight carves it's path across the water.
Long and outstretched it may reach a foreign land
before night turns into day.

The Black Cat

Sleek and silky
Eyes piercing
Whiskers like radar
Sat on the mat.

Skiddaw

Making our ascent the path was steep
the colour of the mountains beautiful in the spring sunshine.
Cloud covered the top of the fells giving the summits an air of
mystery.

Keswick and Derwent Water could be seen in the distance.
Getting smaller the higher we climbed
the wind was howling and very cold
I felt warm with all the exertion.

The path was well trodden leading us further up the fell.
Many people out walking making their way to the summit
as we approached the top, the path levelled off
I was glad of the respite from the constant climb.
3000 feet to the top of the fell the wind so strong we could hardly
stand.

Ancient Woodland

Bluebells distinctive in the spring
vibrant blue purple flowers carpet the woodland floor.
A beautiful purple haze and sweet smell.
Special flowers full of springtime magic.
Wild Garlic accompanies the Bluebells
green leaves and white flowers giving off a pungent smell.
The sign of an ancient woodland.

Bees can be seen retrieving the nectar from the flowers.
A cool wind blows gently.
The wood shady in parts although shafts of sunlight filter through.
Moss covered branches lie on the ground.
Fungi can be seen growing on a few trees
The sights and sounds of the woodland on a perfect spring day.

Spring

Walks delight senses
Old friends return
Frogs and toads spawn
Nature's confetti fills the air.
March hares boxing in the fields
Bumble bees and butterflies venture forth
Woodland wild flowers bloom
Days are longer
Animals awaken
Birdsong peaks.

Birker Fell

Birker fell an upland wilderness
Nothing but the moaning wind can be heard.
Hardy Herdwick sheep graze on the fell oblivious to the noise.
Green bracken grows abundantly.

Mountains erupt into the landscape on the horizon.
The sun has disappeared behind thick white cloud
The mountains which surround me are breathtaking.
Between the crags flow small becks.

I sit and listen to the wind.
I see a ray of sunlight lighting up part of the fell
So beautiful and somehow surreal.
Not another soul about but I do not feel lonely
I feel at peace and happy here.

Changing Light

The green fields spattered with fingers of yellow sunshine
the bare oak tree prominent in the field
some of the branches highlighted by the sun.
Dark clouds gather although some blue sky can be seen.

Beauty surrounds me on this spring morning
I feel so lucky to be alive.
Now the oak tree looks orange and red in parts so beautiful in the
sun.
The changing light and changing moods of the countryside.

Sunkenkirk Stone Circle

Standing alone on a small plateau of land
55 stones stand in a circle.
A keen wind blows across the fells.
Bright and sunny, a beautiful spring day.

The countryside looks fresh and new.
Stone walls covered in moss surrounded by lush green grass
ewes and their lambs lying in the stone circle bathing in the sun.

Thousands of years have past
The stones standing the test of time, some large, some small,
All having a purpose for being there
Rituals held here amongst ancient people
Set in an amphitheatre of fells
A calm and peaceful place where the views just go on and on.

On a Beautiful Spring Morning

Walking up the hill
on a beautiful spring morning
I hear the birds chirping and the whispering of the wind.

The vibrant yellow of the oil seed rape
in the fields catches my eye.
The hill seems to be lit by yellow
sunshine with the rape growing there.

As I approach the woods I see a lone deer
just standing looking around. I step on
a twig which startles the deer and it runs
away.

SUMMER

Old Corpse Road, Haweswater

Easdale Tarn

Walking up to Easdale tarn
the ground hard from the lack of rain
making walking more difficult.
Herdwick sheep and their young graze near the path
a bright sunny day in June a good day for a walk.

Green bracken growing in abundance on the fell
approaching the top some of the ground is boggy
a haven for flora and insects.
Cotton tail grasses growing in places on the bog.
An unusual plant with it's green stem and white cotton wool like
head.

Sitting on a rock at the edge of the tarn
I can see a group of tadpoles in shallow water
their bodies swollen and tails long.
A little further out in the clear water fish dart back and forth.
A light breeze sends small ripples across the tarn.

An amphitheatre of fells surround the area we are sitting in
the scenery quite stunning.
As we sit and watch a black headed gull
it perches on a nearby rock making no effort to move.
A perfect place to be on a beautiful day.

An Evening Stroll

As I walked along the beach
a beautiful sunset lit up the horizon
and the sea in a most magnificent way.
The colours were breathtaking

The sea dressed in gold looked beautiful
Wet sand bathed in gold and silver as the sun sank lower
I had never seen this sight before
the heat of the day was dying too.
The beach was deserted
I watched the sun sinking below the horizon
and the colours fade into dusk.

Whispers of the Green Oak Woods

Gorgeous green oak woods
tall and strong.
Green foiliage and acorns grow.
Many life forms on fallen boughs
A haven for moses and insects.
A river meanders it's way through the valley
large boulders and stones litter it's course.
Round and smooth eroded over the passage of time.
Crystal clear waters, fish can be seen.
River racing through the valley
It's whispers stay with me forever.

Watendlath

Walking through the woods
the sunlight cascades through the trees.
Fox gloves with their delicate purple flowers are covered in
raindrops.
The woods smell fresh from the early morning rain
large droplets of water drip from the trees
green ferns grow in abundance and cover the woodland floor.

The smell of wild garlic fills my nostrils
moss covered tree stumps a haven for insects.
Emerging from the wood into the light
mist lingers on the mountain tops.
A beck meanders along it's course over large boulders and rocks
Watendlath Tarn is surrounded by a amphitheatre of fells.
Good trout fishing for local fishermen.
A wooden bench by the tarn provides a good resting place
the peace and beauty here is something I will always remember.

Early Morning Mist

Early morning mist
a beautiful day in prospect
Mist clings to the Pennines
like limpets cling to a rock.

Sheep and cows grazing in the fields
As the sun breaks through the cloud
a red and blue hot air balloon can be seen in the sky
gliding across the countryside above the mist.

The beautiful colours of the surrounding area
the fields like patchwork quilts bound together by hedgerows.
Nature bestows it's beauty upon us
come wind, rain or shine.

Summer Solstice

Dawn breaks over the ancient stones
marking mid summer's day
mist clings to the henge
an air of mystery surrounds this sacred site.

The sun yellow and bright rises above the horizon
glimmering through the stones.
The birth of a new day.
Druids and pagans joined together in celebration.

The stones tall and strong
standing like soldiers on parade,
they tower above the crowds of people.
The longest day, now the days will get shorter.
The sun a ball of bright yellow fire.
worshipped through the ages
it aligns itself with the stones
marking the new day dawning.

Haystacks

Ripples across Buttermere
make reflections impossible
a breeze blowing cools the warm air.
The ascent up Haystacks steep
the loose stone making the climb hard.

The green of the surrounding countryside magnificent
so many different shades.
Haystacks surrounded by other fells
it claims a superiority of beauty over the area.

At the top a labyrinth of small peaks
and snake like tracks in the mass of dead heather.
The tarns at the top look inviting in the warm summer sun.
The top of Haystacks is a place to sit and reflect
about the great man himself Alfred Wainwright.
forgetting about the worries of everyday life.

Views across Buttermere and Crummock Water stunning.
The descent down the mountain was trouble free
and a day I will always remember.

High Street

Walking up the steep ridge from Mardale valley
The views surrounding us magnificent.
A clear warm summer's day with blue skies and minimal white cloud.
The path narrow with a sheer drop

A stone wall snakes it's way up the ridge
scree covered fells and rocky crags.
Boggy rich black peaty soil has an abundance of plants and grasses.
As we climbed higher I felt tired and weary the wind ruffled my hair.

The air was fresh and clean and it felt good to be alive.
We soaked up the beauty which seemed to go on forever.
We reached the top where we were on High Street. It was so beautiful.
As we continued walking I felt the warmth of the sun on my body.
The ground was squelchy in places

Lake Windermere could be seen on the horizon the largest of the lakes.
We made our descent down Harter Fell
Reaching a stone shelter we drank tea and rested for a while
we listened to water cascading down the mountainside.
I felt calm and at peace with myself.

Approaching Small Water Tarn the water looked deep and blue almost black.
It was inviting on a warm summer's day.
Peace and tranquillity can be found on these fells
A place of beauty to sit and contemplate life.

High Force Falls

Water cascading over jagged rocks
the sound quite deafening.
Deep muddy brown water
froth forming intricate patterns
Green trees and vegetation line the river banks
Rocks formed millions of years ago
erode with the passage of time.
Green grass covered footpaths
followed by a rocky ascent
to the top of the waterfall.
Juniper bushes and ferns grown in abundance
A feeling of peace and calm here.

Crummock Water

As the sun breaks through the cloud
peace and tranquillity can be found here.
Still water, not a ripple on it's surface.
Reflections of the surrounding mountains seem surreal
dew glistens on the grass in the early morning sun the colours so
vivid and vibrant.

Serpentine tracks twist their way around the lake
some parts boggy and squelchy under foot.
Buzzards screech overhead and glide as they catch the thermals
pebbles on the beaches round and smooth, shaped by the
rhythmical waves lapping up on the shoreline.
The water crystal clear very deep in parts.

Old drift wood lying on the beaches
Large boulders covered in yellow and white lichen scattered
along the shore.
The air is really fresh here.
Lots to see and think about.

The Old Corpse Road

Following the corpse up the old corpse road, we could see looking back our houses looking smaller and smaller.
Mardale valley, surrounded by beautiful fells could be seen in all it's glory.
We used the corpse road to take our dead from the valley to the Abbey at Shap.
A group of eight of us followed the corpse today, all dressed in our Sunday best.
It was a beautiful summer's day and quite hot..
We follow a pony carrying the corpse wrapped in a shroud over the top of the mountain.
The ascent up the old road was slow as the path was narrow and the incline steep
The path became rocky and hard going underfoot.
I feel a slight breeze on my face and I stop for a couple of minutes to get my breath. The other's had also stopped.
The sun was beating down on us and there was no shade on the fell.
We walked through the white Cotton Tail grasses found on more boggy areas.
We could see the heat haze hanging over Swindale Valley.
The descent down was steep and it was tricky to hold your footing.
A beck with it's crystal clear waters meanders it's way through the valley.
We could hear the waterfall at Swindale head.
It felt like we had been walking forever, I was thirsty and in need of a rest.
We still had a way to walk.
The afternoon clouds swallow the sun as we approach Shap Abbey.
My skirt hem dark with mud and my shoes are oozing with peaty brown water.
The burial takes place and we start to make the journey home weary and tired.
Hopefully we will get home before darkness falls.

Mel

Meticulously washing her silk like fur her pink tongue going like a piston
She pauses before making circular movements with her paw washing her face gently.
Her long white whisker's twitching with each movement.
Washing over and over her ears sometimes turning them inside out.
Her sinuous tail flicks gently all the while.
Once this washing process is complete she curls up purring softly and is soon asleep.

Orton Scar

An early morning walk to the limestone pavements of Orton Scar
It's a glorious summer's day.
The Lakeland mountains can be seen in the distance
from the top by the monument which marks the summit.

A warm breeze blows across the landscape.
I sit on a limestone rock listening to the curlews calling and the
wind whispeing.
There is an array of wild plants inhabiting deep crevices of the
limestone.
Wild orchids growing in the grass purple in colour and very
dainty.
Sheep graze on the rough grass.
I feel at peace here as the warmth of the sun penetrates my
bones.

Blencathra

Ascending up Blease fell on a cool summer's morning.
We started to climb Blencathra.
A path cut deep through the bracken snaked it's way up the fell side.
The ascent is steep but as the path rises the views looking back are stunning.

A glimmer of sunlight lights up nearby mountains.
A dark cloud sinking down lies low over us.
Sheep graze on the mountain and don't seem worried by our presence.
The path becomes even steeper with green grass giving way to stones and rocks.

Taking a breather for 5 minutes to look at the magnificent views.
We could clearly see Keswick Derwent Water and Cat Bells as well as all the surrounding fells.
A strong westerly wind is blowing.

The summit was disappointing with no cairn in sight.
The rain fell and the wind blew I felt cold and I was shivering.
On our descent we saw a sheep standing near the edge being highlighted by the sunlight with glorious back drop of Lakeland mountains. Just perfect.

Sitting on a rock listening to the wind howling drinking tea soaking up the views.
My thoughts are calm I can think clearly and I am at peace with the world.

Beautiful Rose

Beautiful Rose against the wall
your fragrance pure and new
a droplet sits upon your leaf
Of early morning dew.

After the Rain

Grass seems greener
Air feels cleaner
Roads look wet
Flowers seem vibrant
Rainbows fade
Clouds disappear
Look outside.

The Magnificent Sunset

As I walked along the beach
a beautiful sunset, lit up
the horizon and the sea
in a most magnificent way.

The colours were breathtaking
I called your name, with the
sea dressed in gold. I wanted
so much for you to see it. But
you did not answer, I called
again but all I could hear were
the waves crashing along the
shore.

The wet sand was bathed
in gold and silver, as the sun sank
lower. I had never before seen such
beauty. The heat of the day was
dying too. The beach deserted, I sat
on some rocks and watched the sun go down.
slowly sinking beyond the horizon
and the colours fading into dusk.

Nine Standards

Leaving Kirby Stephen on a beautiful summer's morning,
walking through the streets down to the river Eden
It was cool and fresh.
Following the river we came to dew covered fields.
The dew was heavy and glistening in the sun.
The track was steep passing the quarry, sheep grazed nearby.
As we continued we passed a lot of gorse bushes and thistles
bees were busy collecting nectar.
The music of the wind along with the birds singing was all we
could hear.
The wild moorland was wet and boggy thick dark peaty soil
everywhere.
We sat on a boulder and drank tea admiring the view across the
Vale of Eden.
The vista was so clear the Lakeland fells could be seen in the
distance.
Three hang gliders soared in the air catching thermals so
gracefully.
Nine Standards is on the coast to coast route and is walked by
many fellow walkers.
There was a point where the cairns disappeared from view
making them seem further away.
The summit was near.
Nine imposing cairns lined the summit plateau.
No one knows what they are or how long they have been there,
Tall stone structures.
I sat and listened to the wind, a shiver ran down my spine, it was
chilly and goose bumps covered my skin.
I was totally blown away by the beauty which surrounded me.
I could have sat there forever, totally oblivious to everyday
problems.
Just another day in paradise.

AUTUMN

Grey Crag, Grasmere

Fog

Fog clings to the countryside
the sun trying to peep through.
Everywhere is covered in heavy dew
leaves weeping from the trees
covering the ground in a profusion of autumn colour.

Spider's webs hang like pieces of wet lace
decorated intricately with early morning dew.
Lots of berries in the hedgerows
providing wildlife with an abundance of food.

As time progresses the fog begins to lift
more of the countryside can be seen
the sun covering the land with brightness.

Loch Ness

Loch Ness is a beautiful freshwater lake
the largest in the British Isles.
It is surrounded by beauty
the sun makes the autumn colours look stunning
reds golds browns and oranges
light up the edges of the lake and go on for miles.
Deep water ripples on the surface
as a breeze blows waves to the shoreline.
It is peaceful here
Today I see no monster
tomorrow who knows.

Haweswater Reservoir

Haweswater Reservoir is in the valley of Mardale
The sun dancing over the high fells catching crags
and sun light sometimes sparkling on the water.
A rugged area of high fells fast flowing streams and native
woodland.

The path meanders it's way along the side of the reservoir
plenty of places to stop and admire the view.
Sitting on a large boulder I sit and listen to the sound of the
waves lapping onto the shore.
The sound of the wind and the sheep bleating in the distance can
be heard.

Sheep graze on the lush green grass of the fell side.
When the sun breaks through the cloud it is warm on my face.
Stone foot bridges over Lakeland streams and waterfalls make
crossing easy.
Peace and tranquillity can be found in the Mardale Valley

Hawkeshead

Mist lingers in the valley at Hawkeshead
clinging to it's buildings.
An air of mystery and intrigue surrounds this.
A damp October morning the sun peeping through the cloud
autumn colours stunning.
Spider's webs on gate posts covered in dew hang like wet lace
so stunning in the sun.

The walk to Tarns Hows so beautiful.
Toadstools growing in the woodland on the way.
A red squirrel crosses my path scurrying in the fallen leaves.
Conkers lying on the path empty spiky shells near by.
Buzzards screech above us a real piercing eerie sound.
We stand quietly and listen.

Rain drops and Rainbows

Rain: Some days it rains all day and would seem it was never going to stop.
Even the ducks on the Lake are wet.
Trees shed their leaves, the rain helps them on their way.
Rain, Rain go away and maybe return another day.
The sun starts to peep from behind a cloud, the rain finally stops making way for the most beautiful rainbow.
I looked at it in awe and could see the most vibrant colours.
Where were the ends of the Rainbow?
Was there a pot of gold, anywhere in sight, like the old wives tales suggest?
I liked the bold blue colour and the warm orange.
You could almost feel the warmth, on this chilly autumn day.
Smelling the dampness around me, I looked up again,
only to find the rainbow had disappeared into thin air and no pots of gold were ever found.

Coniston

Rhythmical waves lap against along the shores edge.
Debris is littered along the shoreline
A battered tree stands in solitude it's roots exposed
The tree in autumn colour looks stunning in the sun.
Mountains stand mighty and serene like fortresses in the night.
Yellow and pink buoys break the monochromatic greyness of the water
The sky dark over the mountainside
Speed boats roar in the distance breaking up the peace and tranquillity of Coniston

Great Carrs

On a beautiful morning walking up the fell side
squelching mud underfoot
Herdwick sheep grazing covered in blue and red paint
moving quickly as we approach.

The views of the surrounding fells spectacular.
As we walk to the top we can see the memorial with it's cross just
below the summit.
It is dedicated to eight airmen who lost their lives on the fell.
Mist was present when the plane crashed.
Aircraft parts strewn across the mountain.

Sitting by the monument a sense of peace prevails
A wooden cross sits on top of the stone cairn
covered in remembrance poppies to remember the men.
A wonderful place to sit and enjoy the stillness.

Sun and Moon

A deep red glow from a sinking sun illuminates the sky
Some dramatic sunsets during the autumn months
Summer seems a distant memory now
warm summer days giving way to crisp cool nights.
As dusk falls, the countryside is still and silent.
The moon big and full carves it's way through the darkness
only to disappear as the sun rises.

Sunset in October

Reds golds and oranges
of this October sunset
paint a picture on the horizon
sea shimmering effortlessly
in the dappled light.
Gulls flying low
catching fish before the sun drops below the horizon.
A chilly wind blows
A reminder that winter is near.

Down besides the River Dee

Down by the river golden pine needles carpet the paths
Green mosses lie in abundance soft and spongy under foot.
A red squirrel scurries across our path it stops and forages for
food.
Many different species of toadstool grow on this damp and earthy
ground
Toadstools red with white spots stand out against the lime green
moss.
Dead trees scattered along the river bank.
Cold waters of the Dee clear and fast flowing.
Collections of large stones litter the river course.
Heavy rains and fast flowing water carry the rocks down stream.
A dull day with a light breeze perfect for a woodland walk.

A walk around Tomintoul Scotland

We walk through some woods
I see and abundance of red Rowan berries
hanging in clumps on bare trees.
A strange lichen silvery grey in colour called Old Man's Beard
creeps along the branches of many species of trees.
It looks eerie and unreal.
The wood is damp from recent rains
dead leaves decaying underfoot
toadstools grow by the path pale brown with white gills
A little robin sits on a branch attracting our attention.
It's red breast and brown feathers distinctive.
The sun cascades through the trees brightening our path as we
walk.

From the car window

Sunlight bursts through the dark cloud
picking up the varying shades of green.
Fields fit neatly together
like squares on a patchwork quilt bound by stone walls.
Walls that have stood the test of time.

An old mine stands on the fell side
The Pennine moorland is rough
No trees or shrubs to be seen
sheep roam freely eating scrub grass.
A vista that changes with the seasons.

Autumn's Glory

A beautiful sunrise
on this autumn morning
colours stunning.
Reds golds, yellows and oranges
the sun blinding as it rises,
autumn colours highlighted
pink clouds drifting effortlessly across a blue sky.
As I sit here and watch
a moment in time is captured.
The whispering of the wind can be heard
autumn leaves weeping from the trees
scattering on damp ground.
Soon everything will hibernate for a few months.
Nature will take a long sleep
preparing for the energy of spring.

WINTER

Cat Bells, Derwent Water

Harter Fell

Walking up Gatescarth pass to the summit of Harter Fell
the only sound that could be heard
are birdsong and water cascading over the rocks.
The ascent to the top was steep
patches of snow lay along the ridge,

A gentle breeze blowing
stone cairns stand at the summit constructed of stone and
twisted metal.
The views from here go on and on.
A cloudy day but rays of sunshine appear now and then
lighting up surrounding fells.

The path down to Small Water Tarn narrow.
A stone built shelter can be seen on the way down
sheltering many people from wind and rain.
The stone on the path loose making walking difficult.
Men hunting deer on the lower levels.
Haweswater looking as beautiful as ever.

Allonby Cumbria

The waves on the Solway Firth
come crashing onto the shore.
White foam picked up by the moaning wind
is deposited on the beach.
A lone windsurfer sails the sea
over the waves back and forth
he struggles to hold on.
The sea turns brown
a storm is brewing
the sky has gone heavy the clouds will burst.
Scottish mountains can be seen across the firth
out to the Northwest white wispy clouds appear
I see a rainbow in all it's glory
the ends I cannot follow.

Desolate Shores

Waves hit desolate shores
wind howling around the cliffs
white foam clumps on the beach
December is a bleak time
think of the spring
remember the good times.

Sunrise

It's dark
the sun has not yet woken
from it's slumbers of the night.
Slowly the dawn breaks
And after a while the sun rises
the sun glows and being winter it is low in the sky
Everyday the cycle is repeated.

Friar's Crag

Solitude is what I feel here
peace and tranquillity within
Mountains covered in snow
making the vista look clean and sterile
Derwent Water frozen in parts
Canada geese and ducks sitting on the ice
in the early morning sun.
Mountains reflected beautifully in the still water
Fresh cold crisp air fills my lungs this frosty morning
Grey stone steps twinkle in the sunlight.
The little beach scattered with dead leaves and twigs crunch
under my feet
This is a beautiful place and I long to stay.

Angletarn Pikes

Mountains stand in all their glory
snow capped peaks at higher levels
white snow reflecting beautiful sunlight.
Shades of green on the lower fells
A real contrast from the brilliant white.
Walking up the path stunning beauty surrounds me
I stop and look at the view
there is dark cloud behind me
shafts of sunlight cascading down.
A contrast to the beautiful sight in front of me.
As I climbed higher the scree underfoot became loose.
Reaching the top, low cloud descended .
It was wet underfoot and muddy
Angle Tarn shrouded in mist.
I sat on a rock and drank tea thinking about what I had seen.
Remnants of the snow remain here
The wind was cold making me shiver.
Mist returned covering the tarn.
The air fresh and clean.
Walking back towards the sunlight
I stood on top and looked around me.
On this February day I was glad to be alive
The beauty of these Lakeland fells will stay with me forever.

Castlerigg Stone Circle

A peaceful atmospheric place
Castlerigg Stone Circle covered in snow
with the beautiful backdrop of the Lakeland mountains.
Thirty eight stones stand in the circle.
some large some small standing the test of time.
Thousands of years have passed
many seasons have gone by

A magical place especially in winter time
surrounded by snow covered mountains
The sun shinning through the broken cloud giving the fells a
romantic glow.
The cold penetrates my bones while I stand and contemplate.
This will always be a special place.

A River runs through it

Mountains stand in all their glory
stretching as far as the eye can see.
Snow clad peaks so lily white
wait until spring to disappear.
The air crisp in the valley
as a river flows over the rocks and boulders.
Like ballerinas dancing on a stage
the winter sun strong and penetrating.
Snow melts in the valley
trees drip with the ice melt
as it falls on sodden ground.

Winter Magic

Jack Frost worked his magic everything white and frozen
cobwebs so delicately placed adorn the bushes in the garden
hanging limp and glistening in the sun.
No spiders to be seen.
As the sun gets higher in the sky the frost melts and glistening
diamonds disappear into an abyss of nothingness.
The green grass, muddy underfoot becomes a haven for worms.
Birds scavenge on this winter's day for food.
Frozen ground still solid in the shade.
Smoke rising up from the abundant chimneys
no wind just stillness surrounds the area and silence envelops.

Darkness

A pale moon up in the sky
lost souls of loneliness weeping sad tears
two lovers entwined in a deep oblivion.
A man of the road huddles in the doorway trying to
keep warm.
Bare trees in the moonlight silent and still.
Let the hours of darkness pass to let the light in.

Easedale Tarn

Icy paths slippery underfoot
meander through rocky crags
climbing up to Easedale Tarn.
Frosted leaves lying on frozen ground
water cascading over jagged rocks
Quite deafening to the listening ear.
Herdwick sheep search for patches of unfrozen grass
The sun hiding behind dull cloud
The tarn still, mountains reflected in the water seem surreal.

Thundery Skies

Angry thunderous sky of grey
white waves pound desolate shores
Roaring like tormented lions
white foam rushing amongst rocky crags
for a moment in time
before the tide ebbs away.

A Winter's day

A cold wind blows this early February morning
pink clouds like giant candy floss float across a beautiful sky.
Large puddles in the road from heavy winter rains.
New born lambs a few days old nestle into the sides of their
mother's to keep warm.
Snow drops adorning many roadside banks
their dainty bells of white so delicate.
Soon the season will change and spring will arrive.
New life and new beginnings.

20735027R00037

Printed in Great Britain
by Amazon